The Glory of God's Divine Protection

Children Are Blessed Like a Tree Planted by the Water

Janice P. Manous

Acknowledgments

I thank the Lord Jesus for giving me the wisdom to write this book. I thank Kenneth Manous my husband for always supporting me in everything I do. I thank my family for allowing me to share their experiences and stories of how God has blessed them with divine protection. I thank Pastor R.W. Townsend, Pastor S. Paul Courtney, & Pastor Ray Pickett for their support. I thank my children Kenneth, Shaunte, Joe, Kim, Shannon, Jamie, Obie, Nicole, Gary, family and friends for praying and interceding on my behalf to complete this book.

Foreword

This book will awaken your heart to the fact that God has a plan for all of us and we can fulfill our purpose if we pray and have faith in him to guide us through everyday situations. When you read these true stories, you know that prayer is what got us through. Our mom has always had a hunger for God's word. That is a generation blessing. You can see that our family has stood on God's word through all these short stories in this book. This book will take you on a spiritual journey of how God brought us to victory in every situation.

Kenneth D. Manous
Shannon Manous Pope
Jamie Manous Hanks

"Trust God and Pray about it", Most believers say it but Janice Manous shares her experiences revealing a child, a women, a mother, and a Grammy that truly trust God for everything. Through Godly living a powerful and fervent prayer life, Janice reveals the beauty and blessed life of a believer in everyday events. Those who share her faith will find common ground. Those that don't will find higher ground.

Pastor S. Paul Courtney
Senior Pastor Bethlehem Baptist Church
Author: "Kingdom Moments"

Table of Contents

Introduction

SPEAK BLESSINGS OVER YOUR CHILD EVERY DAY

To bring life to anything, you must speak your situations into existence. Speak by faith these words for and with your children every day before they leave you. God's favor, blessings, and supernatural power will guide them.

- I am a child of the Most High God and I belong to Jesus.
- I have wisdom knowledge and common sense.
- I can do all things through Jesus Christ.
- I put on the whole armor of God to withstand anything that will come against me.
- I listen to the Holy Spirit.
- I am safe from all hurt, harm and danger.
- I do not have the spirit of fear but of love, power and a sound mind.
- I am smart. I make sound decisions, and God's supernatural grace will cover me.
- I will have a great day in Jesus' name.

1. 1982 The Glory of God and Many Miracles

We moved to Texas many years ago from Tulsa Oklahoma. I enjoyed living in Tulsa. I thought it was the ideal place to live and raise a family. We both had good jobs. We loved our church and we had many good friends there. We had three children (Joe, Kenneth Damian, and Shannon). I went to my new Dr. in Tulsa, Oklahoma thinking I would have a complete physical and maybe get some type of birth control. He told me I was pregnant. I had been sick, and I was very happy to hear the good news and to learn why I had been feeling tired. Kenn and I were very excited. This was a miracle. Everything was going great. I was teaching first grade and I enjoyed going to work every day. To top it off we were going to have another baby.

A few months later my sister Diannah who was an Elementary school teacher was killed at her school in Oklahoma City. There was an explosion in the room behind the cafeteria. A hot water broiler blew up when she was on duty in the cafeteria. She and six other children were killed. Her ten-year-old daughter Shavonya Nickole was in the cafeteria at that time but she said her face was turned away from her mom and she didn't see her mom get hurt. A student next to her also died that day. But God blessed our family when her life was spared. That was another blessing and miracle. She and many children were sent to the hospital. Nicole later learned from her dad that her mom had died. Many prayers were prayed for her and we still pray for her every day. She is my God daughter, so it was then that she became one of my children. This tragedy was on every news station. My dad Jesse Pettus was on his way home when he heard about the explosion on the radio. He pulled over and prayed for the parents and families of the teacher and the children who had died, not knowing that he was praying for himself, my mom Valaska, and my siblings Roscoe, Norma, Terry, Rita, Diannah and me. I was the teacher on playground duty at my school in Tulsa, Oklahoma when my staff was talking about this tragedy. I didn't get the message until I got home that afternoon. God knew it would be hard for me, so he protected me by not letting me hear it at school. That was another miracle. It was a very hard time for my family. Having parents who loved God and had faith in him was the biggest blessing and miracle we could have. My Dad said that he knew it was her time to go be with Jesus because God does not make mistakes. It was not our choice, but God has a reason for everything he does, and we just must trust him. Our job is to be there and pray for Nickole, tell her stories about her mom, and to always have faith in God no matter what. In listening to the wonderful things that were said about Diannah after she died, I almost think she knew. She had everything in order. She was the choir director of her choir at church. She had made corsages by hand for every member of her choir for a recent musical. The choir wore those corsages the day of the funeral. I remember asking her if she needed help making all the flowers, and she said," Oh no, I enjoy doing this." I then said," that's a lot of work." My brother in law Raymond Pickett who is full of wisdom said, "Let her get her blessings the way she wants." She blessed many people in her life time. It was a miracle having her for a sister for thirty-two years. Her life was a blessing to us. Nicole has been a wonderful blessing to our family. She had a hard time growing up without Diannah, but God held her hand, and ordered her steps. By grace and God's blessings she grew up to be the beautiful lady God intended her to be. She grew up with many mothers. We tell her stories about her mom all the time. It's so amazing that she is a lot like her mom. I thank God for generational blessings. Nickole Is now married to Gary and they have two boys, Kendrae and LaRay. She has seen many miracles in her lifetime.

A few months passed, and it was time for me to have my baby. We were excited and couldn't wait to see her. I had a cesarean child birth just like I did with all my other children. She was so beautiful! I talked with my new Dr. and he had some disturbing news to tell Ken and me. He said that my last Dr. had sewed my intestines to my incision when he had delivered Shannon. When he went to deliver Jamie, he cut right into my intestates. After he delivered Jamie, he had to do major surgery to correct what my old Dr. had done. He also said that Jamie was a miracle baby. If she had not come along, I may have soon died because of the severity of this problem. All I could say was THANK YOU LORD!

Kenneth and I had many miracles that year. We had our beautiful new baby and our wonderful children at home. My God baby Nickole was now one of my children. Last, I am still here so I have my life to thank God for! OH WHAT A GOD WE SERVE! We serve a God who provides miracles seen and unseen every day for us and our children. Thank You Lord!

Scriptures:

John 14:1-3
Let not your heart be troubled: ye believe in God, believe also in me. In my Father's house are many mansions: if it were not so, I would have told you. I go to prepare a place for you. And if I go and prepare a place for you, I will come again and receive you unto myself; that where I am there ye may be also.

Psalm91:1
"He that dwelleth in the secret place of the most-high shall abide under the shadow of the Almighty"

2 Timothy 1:7
For God hath not given us the spirit of fear; but of power, and of love, and of a sound mind.

Prayer:

Dear Heavenly Father,
We love you so much. We ask for forgiveness for all our sins. We declare that we dwelleth in the secret place of our most high God. We ask that you remove any thought in our heart that is not of you. We declare that every member of our family is saved. Thank you for carrying us through every situation that we face and for the seen and unseen miracles you do for us every day. Thank you for saturating every part of our children and family with your grace, mercy and precious blessings. I thank you that my family walks in your eternal light and not in darkness. We will trust you in every decision you make for us. We know that everything works for the good for those who love and have faith in you. Thank you for keeping us in perfect peace. Amen

2. The First Three Minutes

God gives us many blessings every day. Sometimes we are so busy that we don't see all his blessings. One day Kenneth Damian, Shaunte, and my granddaughter Carrington flew home to see us. When I saw them, my heart filled with joy. We hugged and kissed and when I looked at Carrington, she looked me in my eyes and her sweet voice said "HELLO GRAMMY, HOW ARE YOU TODAY"? Wow, her voice was like a breath of fresh air. She made me feel so special. It is so important to make the first three minutes of seeing someone very important by focusing all your attention on them and just making them feel like they are special and deserving of your love and praise. When you try to make someone feel special, it will return to you. I now make it a point when I see my children, to give them three minutes of special attention. You can learn a lot from them in three minutes. We went to California to see my son Joe and Kim. Their son Little Joe saw us when we got in the car at the airport. I made sure to give him three minutes of special attention. He is younger, but he could feel the love in our conversation and kisses.

My mom once said that if your children have five people in their life besides their parents that are interested in them and their well-being, they are likely to be very successful. Those special people can be aunts, uncles, sister's brothers, grandparents, god parents and friends. Make a point to be that special person in someone's life. Spend some time talking to that person. Remind them that God is always there with them to help them make decisions. Pray with and for them and let them know that they always have your support and love.

Scriptures:

Romans 16:16
Salute one another with a holy kiss. The churches of Christ salute you.

Matthew 18:19
Again, I say unto you, that if two of you shall agree on earth as touching anything that they shall ask, it shall be done for them of my father, which is in heaven.

Prayer

Dear Heavenly Father,
Thank you for all the blessings you give us every day. Please forgive us for all our sins if we have done or said anything that was not pleasing to you. You have graced every one of us with talents to do great things. Please help my children to discover all the gifts and talents you have for them. Thank you for blessing my children and helping them so see their self-worth. Thank you for saving them by your grace. I love and praise you Father. Thanks for being there for us and never leaving us. Thank you for my children.
Amen

3. Our Children Are Blessed With Hidden Talents

Our children are born with many talents. Some talents come natural for them. Have you ever heard someone say," Oh she has a natural talent for (example) writing, reading, speaking, singing, dancing, cheerleading, football, basketball, and the list goes on."

Some of their talents have to be developed. One spring day, my son Kenneth Damian was asked to speak for our children's honors day at our church. He was a senior in high school at that time. He had never been asked to do a formal speech in front of a group this large before. I remember him telling us that he felt happy he was asked to speak but he had some fears and insecurities about doing it. His dad told him that sometimes you have to step out in faith to do things you have never done before. We read the scripture in II Timothy chapter one verse seven and discussed it. We told him that God has given us everything we need inside to do amazing things. Then we sat down together and wrote out his speech. He read it many times. The more he read, the more confident he got. He did an amazing job on his speech a few weeks later. After it was all over, he felt so good. He had discovered other talents that God had put inside of him. This opportunity prepared him for the next level that God had for him. When opportunities come and we decide we can't do it because of fear, we limit the treasures that God has stored inside of us. God wants us to be victorious in everything we do. When we have Jesus we inherit everything we need to complete our destiny in life. Fear will try to stop our children, but when they think victory in Jesus, they become winners for life.

Scripture:

2 Timothy 1:7
For God hath not given us the spirit of fear; but of power, and of love, and of a sound mind.

Prayer

Dear Heavenly Father,
Thank you Lord for my children. Please forgive us of all our sins. Father we come to you speaking your word into my children. "For God hath not given us the spirit of fear; but of power, and of love, and of a sound mind." My children will discover everything you have put inside of them. They will not fear but have victory in every opportunity you place before them. We know that if they think it, they can do it. Help me to encourage them to have confidence, and remind them that if they seek you, nothing will be impossible unto them. I love you Lord. Amen

4. There Will Always Be Storms

All of us have been in a thunder storm. When we see the storm clouds coming up we start talking about it. We need to prepare by getting inside and taking cover. If we are driving, we pull off the road at the next exit or try to beat it by driving out of it. With storms there come many things like lightning, tornadoes, blizzards, thunder, dark sky, floods, snow, sleet, and ice. We take cover because we really don't know what that storm will bring. Our house, and our cars can be flooded or damaged. Hail stones can hurt people, or our property. Sleet and snow can cause hazard driving conditions. Tornadoes can up root everything and take it away. The rain falling outside can have a peaceful sound. Then all of a sudden you see lightning and hear a loud thunder sound like fire crackers. When the storm is moving on, you can still hear the rain drops outside but the rowing thunder sounds seem to be moving away in the distance. Soon the rain stops and the storm is over. There is a peace that comes over you. You start praising God that the storm is over. Sometimes we see a beautiful rainbow in the sky to let us know that the storm is over. We look out to see if there is any damage. Then the clouds move away and we can see the sunlight in the day peeping threw the straggly clouds. For a while we see water on the ground and puddles here and there to remind us that God has a reason for everything. While he is taking care of the grass and flowers outside, he is also taking care of us inside. Our life is full of storms. Some are more devastating than others. Families experience short storms every day. The problems and decisions we make every day have its consequences. Then there are the big storms that last more than a day. It can go into days, months, and maybe years to overcome. Sometimes we wonder if the storm will ever end.

God assures us that the storms in our life will end. All he asks of us is to trust him and have faith threw it all. Storms can upset us to the point that we can't see the outcome or if there will be a rainbow. Sometimes the hurt and pain is so deep, we can't see or hear the storm moving away. It seems that it's on top of us and the thunder and lightning is constant. Our emotions are clouding our happy ending. Some people give up and feel their life is over for happiness. They feel defeated and heart broken. Instead of trying to move out of the storm, their thinking moves them deeper into the storm and they give up completely. Some people blame the very person who wants us to succeed God, for their mistakes and decisions. This disappoints God. We belong to him. He is our Lord and Savior, Our Father. No parent wants their children to fail. The bible has the answer to every problem we could possibly have. That's why we pray for wisdom, knowledge, and common since every day. God wants the best for us. He will fight with you but you have to fight for yourself. There is no problem too big for Him. We are God's chosen people. That means we inherent his goodness mercy and grace. His blessings are there for the asking. God can forgive any and everything we do. When we ask for forgiveness he will throw our sins in the deepest ocean and forget. All he asks of us is that we trust him and forgive ourselves. Healing comes when we forgive ourselves and others. Forgiveness is the key. If God can forgive us our many sins every day, surly we can forgive others who knowingly and unknowingly hurt us. After we forgive self, we than sit and write down goals, which is a plan to get out of that storm. Stop replaying negative thoughts in your mind to keep you in the storm. Look at your goals constantly to remind yourself to stay on that road to recovery and move away from the storm. Children of God never give up. Your partner is the Holy Spirit. He guides and helps you through every day. Jesus lives in you so you are never alone. He is going threw it with you. You are never alone. The difference between success and failure is Faith in God. It doesn't matter how big or small the storm, you have to keep your mind on God. Praise him for your outcome. Problems will way you down. Give them to God. He is more than enough to make you a winner. Put your faith in him and you will see a rainbow every time. He said if we have the faith of a tiny mustard seed than we can move mountains. How simple is that? Right? Thanks be to God who always causes us to triumph. God wants us to talk to him about everything. If we are silent we can hear his answer every time. Rainbows and blessings are a lot alike. They both come from God. They make us feel better. They put our hearts and soul at rest so the stress is gone. We are an overcomer in Christ Jesus. Problems come and go, but the biggest problem of all is not learning from them or changing our behavior. Great are the afflictions of the righteous, but our God will deliver us out of all of them.

We can always recover from a storm if we give it to God and don't take it back. Thank him every day because rainbows are gifts. Keep believing in God and he will keep blessing you and your family.

5. Angels Were Watching

One evening my husband packed up to go to Singapore on business for the computer company he worked for. My children and I took him to the airport. When we made it home, everyone got ready for bed. Before we went to bed, all of us prayed together that God would bless and watch over their dad while he was away. Then we asked that God would watch over us while we were sleep and that he would send his angels to surround our home and keep us from all danger. After the children were asleep, I thanked God for watching over us all and prayed that we would get the rest we needed for the next day. I also prayed that Kenneth would make it to Singapore safely and that God's protection would be over him the whole trip. I went to bed around ten o'clock and quickly feel asleep. I woke up around two o'clock in the morning. I checked the children, thanked God for watching over us, and checked to make sure all our doors were locked. I went back to my bedroom and went to bed. I tossed and turned but could not get back to sleep. I prayed to fall asleep because I knew I had to get up early to the next day. I kept reminding God to help me fall asleep so I wouldn't be tired the next day. Then I heard a truck drive down the alley behind my house. As I laid there I noticed that the sound of the truck never left. In fact it sounded like it was right behind my house. I got out of bed and walked to the kitchen. It was then that my garage door started going up. I quickly went to the alarm system and pressed the panic button. As I was talking to the 911 operator I went to Kenneth Jr.'s room and asked him to go to the girl's room and get in the bed with them. Their bedroom was by my room. I went back to the kitchen as I talked with 911. The lady told me to go to the back door next to the garage and open it. There was a police officer waiting for me. I was so happy he had come in two and a half minutes. He told me that my car window had been broken and stuff was stolen from my car. Glass was everywhere. He asked me to pull the car into the Garage.

He also told me that several houses in my neighborhood had been broken into and hopefully they would catch them soon. About a month later I found out that they had arrested the three men. After the officer left, I got on my knees and thanked God for taking good care of us. I went to the bedroom where my children were still sleeping. I went back to bed and quickly feel asleep. The next day I told my children how God had taken good care of us and had kept us from danger like we prayed. His angels kept guard over our doors and kept them from coming into our home. Satan had come to hurt us but our faith in God protected us from him and his attacks. I thank God for his word and his love for us.

Scriptures:

Psalm 56:11
In God have I put my trust: I will not be afraid what man can do unto me.

Psalm 91:10-11
There shall no evil befall thee, neither shall any plague come nigh thy dwelling.
For he shall give his angels charge over them, to keep thee in all thy ways.

Timothy 1:7
For God hath not given us the spirit of fear; but of power, and of love, and of a sound mind.

Prayer:

Dear Heavenly Father,
Lord we praise you and we thank you for keeping us safe at all time. We thank you that we can pray for our children and leave it with you knowing that you will keep them safe. Thank you for keeping us in perfect peace when we have faith in you and your word. Please forgive us for all of our sins and help us to forgive others who have hurt us. We pray for them that they are saved. Lord we love and praise you. Blessed be the Lord my father and savior. Amen

6. Breathe Grammy

Feelings are a part of life. In a day, we can experience many different feelings and emotions. We can also experience more than one feeling at the same time. Anger is a normal human feeling. It is not a bad thing to get angry, but it is important that we know how to handle it. One day my granddaughter Lauren and I decided to make a pound cake. As I was gathering our ingredients, she reached up on top of the counter and pulled down a bag of sugar. The bag was open. It fell on the floor and sugar went everywhere. I looked at the sugar and I said," LAUREN!" Four-year-old Lauren looked at me as I was looking at the floor and she quickly said, "BREATH GRAMMY!" I looked at her and we both started to laugh. I was laughing because of her words. She remembered what to do if she were to get angry. She was laughing because I was not angry any more. We cleaned up the sugar and finished the cake. This became one of our family traditions. When Carrington my other granddaughter from Atlanta, and Joseph my grandson from California comes, Lauren, Carrington, Joseph, and I always enjoy making a pound cake together. Sometimes you should laugh to get over being angry. I am an elementary school counselor and I have told many school children who have come to me angry, to breath. I told them to close their mouth, breathe in through their nose, and breathe out through their mouth. The cool air would help their body to calm down. They did this several times. Doing this helped them to relax and to be able to discuss their problem effectively. I also told my children to slowly count to fifteen to help them to get their mind off their problem and calm down. If they were still angry they had to count again. I also would tell them to think of something pleasant to take their mind off what they were angry about.

This would help them to be able to talk about the situation in a calm way and problem solve threw it. Going outside to walk or run or doing some exercises is also a great way for children to relieve stress and tension. Anger is like any other feeling but it is important to recognize it and to keep it under control. This is also a time to talk about forgiveness. I have found that children are so quick to forgive their friend when their friend understands how the disagreement made them feel. They also forget quickly and are ready to go back to playing.

You and your child can talk and pray together about their feelings. Being a good listener with eye to eye contact is a great way for your children to know that you love and care about them and their feelings.

Scripture:

Psalm 37:4
Delight thyself also in the Lord: and he shall give thee the desires of thane heart'

Prayer

Dear Lord,
I thank you that you are a great God and that you love my children. Please forgive us for all our sins. I give my children to you and ask that your blessings be upon them always. They are great upon this earth. They have wisdom, knowledge and common since. I know you have graced them to do great things. Please help my children to have control of all their emotions. Please help them to forgive others who have hurt them. Help them to respect others and that respect and forgiveness is returned to my children. Thank you for your everlasting love. We love you Lord.
Amen

7. Don't Look Back

I was a teenager when I first heard and understood the Bible story about Lot, his wife and daughters. In Genesis chapter 19, is where I read the story of how God destroyed Sodom and Gomorrah. He saved Lot, his wife and their two daughters. There was one part of this story that bothered me. Lot and his family were told to leave the city and not look back. But Lot's wife looked back and she became a pillar of salt. This had to be devastating to her family. It really bothered me that she looked back. I also wondered," what was she thinking?' She lost her life because she didn't obey God. When my children were little, I remember having a problem that I found it hard to get through. I remember praying to God and saying," but God every time I look back I" and that is when he stopped me. His voice was so strong and clear. He said to me, "DON'T LOOK BACK"! Wow! God does not want us to look back on situations that hurt us. He wants us to trust him and move forward. Looking back can hurt us when we don't leave the past in the past. Then I thought about Lot's wife. Looking back can hurt or even destroy you. He wants us to leave the past in the past, forgive and move on. Replaying the past over and over in our minds can stop us from moving forward and receiving the blessings that God has for us. When our children come to us with a problem, God wants us to pray for wisdom and guidance before we discuss the problem so he can speak threw us. We can help them to understand that forgiving helps them to feel better and not block their blessings. Then we pray for the person that hurt them and ask God to give your child peace of mind in this situation. My sisters Norma and Rita were talking with me one day. They reminded me that my mom told them to never look back. You prayed for wisdom and knowledge when you made the decision. You made a good decision. Never second guess yourself when you have prayed. Everything happens for a reason. Trust your judgment and move on. We are not perfect but everything will turn out for our good when we trust God. You can't see yourself to new beginnings if you are looking back.

Scriptures:

Proverbs 3:5-6
Trust in the Lord with all thine heart; and lean not unto thine own understanding. In all thy ways acknowledge him, and he shall direct thy paths.

Mark 11:22-26
And Jesus answering saith unto them, Have faith in God. For verily I say unto you, that whosoever shall say unto this mountain, Be thou removed, and be thou cast into the sea; and shall not doubt in his heart but shall believe that those things which he saith shall come to pass; he shall have whatsoever he saith. Therefore I say unto you, what things so ever ye desire, when ye pray, believe that ye receive them and ye shall have them. And when ye stand praying, forgive, if ye have ought against any; that your Father also which is in heaven may forgive you your trespasses. But if ye do not forgive, neither will your Father which is in heaven forgive your trespasses.

Prayer:

Dear Lord Jesus, We praise you. We thank you that whatever we desire, when we pray and believe we receive them that we shall have them. Please forgive us our trespasses and help us to forgive the people who have hurt us. Also we pray for those who have hurt us. Bless them right now in Jesus' name. We agree that the favor of God go before and bless this situation.

We have faith that you will work out this problem and please bring us all peace of mind. This we ask in Jesus' name we pray. Amen

8. Don't Start Your Day Until You Pray

Our family Slogan is "DON'T START YOUR DAY UNTIL YOU PRAY".

We say it every day as a reminder of who we are and who's we are. We are children of God and we belong to God. God wants us to be specific when we pray. He wants to bring a harvest to our children. My siblings Roscoe, Norma, Terry, Rita, Diannah and I have talked over and over again how important the Lord's Prayer is to us. The first prayer your children should learn is the Lord's Prayer. This is the prayer that Jesus taught his disciples. It is very easy to learn. The Lord's Prayer says it all. God knows what we stand in need of before we pray. There are many blessings included in the Lord's Prayer for your family. My family prays this prayer every morning to start our day. It will take your children no time to learn this prayer. It will bless their day.

Scripture:

Proverbs 3:5-6
Matthew 6:9-13 "Lord's Prayer"
Luke 11:2-3   A shorter version of "Lord's Prayer"

Matthew 6:9-13
After this manner therefore pray ye:

Our Father which art in heaven, Hallowed be thy name. Thy kingdom come. Thy will be done in earth, as it is in heaven. Give us this day our daily bread. And forgive us our debts, as we forgive our debtors.

And lead us not into temptation, but deliver us from evil: For thine is the kingdom, and the power, and the glory, forever. Amen.

9. Forgiveness

Teaching first grade was a blessing. I enjoyed going to work every day. I loved my job, the children, the parents and the people I worked with. My mom and dad (Jesse and Valaska) always told us that you never know love until you give it to others. It returns back to you. I have found that they were right. Children are quick to love and to forgive. I have had children come to me with a problem during recess. Instead of me working it out for them, I found that asking them to sit down and discuss the problem was easier than me trying to solve it for them. They had to agree before they could go play. They quickly solved their problem. They both apologized and ran off to play as if there was never a problem. As children get older, it seems that it is sometimes a little harder to forgive their friends. They worry about what others have said about them and how it made them feel. They replay the situation over and over in their minds and find it hard to forgive or forget. Sometimes they tell us and sometimes we just know by their actions they are sad or worried about something. Try to get them to talk about their day. Listen carefully to let them know that you love and care about them and together try to solve the problem. Just listening helps a lot. Talk with your child about forgiving the person that hurt them. With God's help we can forgive our friends. If we hand the situation over to God, he will help us to forgive. If we hold on to it, then it controls us and our actions. If we forgive others, God will forgive us.

Scripture:

Mark 11:24-26
Therefore I say unto you, what things soever ye desire when ye pray, believe that ye receive them, and ye shall have them. And when ye stand praying forgive, if ye have aught against any: that your Father also which is in heaven may forgive you your trespasses. But if ye do not forgive, neither will your Father which is in heaven forgive your trespasses.

Prayer:

Dear Lord, we love and praise you. We thank you for loving us. Please forgive our sins and help us to forgive the person who has hurt my child. Bless that person. We give it to you knowing you will work this out. We release these hurt feelings to you and are letting them go. We have faith in your word and will not let this hurt us anymore. Thank you for blessing all of us and keeping us in your care.
Amen

10. Get Up and Pray

It was 3:00 a.m. I was wide awake and found that I could not go back to sleep. Has this ever happened to you? I talked with many of my family members and friends and this has happened to them. One night I decided to turn this negative into a positive. I got out of my bed and went into each one of my children's room. I softly placed my hand on their back and prayed for each one of them. The first time I did this, it startled them until they saw me and heard me praying for them. Shannon told me one morning years later that she heard her door open and saw me come in. She said to herself," Oh it is just mom praying for me" and she quickly went back to sleep. Some nights my children never knew I was in their room praying for them. Praying for each child only took a few minutes. I went back to bed and then said a prayer for my husband and myself. I fell asleep after that. I had turned my worry into faith by giving everything to God and resting in him. I thanked him in advance for working everything out. I believed he would take care of everything and he did. God does not want us to worry about anything. If we trust in him and his word, and have faith, HE WILL WORK IT OUT!

Scripture:

John 14:12-14
Verily, verily, I say unto you, He that believeth on me, the works that I do shall he do also; and greater works than these shall he do; because I go unto my Father. And whatsoever ye shall ask in my name, that will I do, that the Father may be glorified in the Son. If ye shall ask any thing in my name, I will do it.

Prayer:

Dear Heavenly Father, I praise you and thank you for all the blessings you have given to us. We love you Lord. We magnify your holy name. Thank you that anything I ask in your name, you will do. I give you all my family's problems and I rest knowing you love my family and will take care of us. We believe your word is your will and we thank you for loving us.
Amen

11. Get Wisdom

Our children desperately need God's word in their heart and great will be their peace. Teach a scripture to your children every week. Put it on the refrigerator. Say it every day with them. This will bring a harvest in their life. Our children will be mighty and make good decisions. That doesn't mean that trouble will not come their way. It does mean that no matter what comes, they will have the keys to problem solve through it and you will have peace when you pray that God is in control. My Mom and Dad would always pray for their six children. They would ask God to bless us with wisdom. Their prayer was that God would open our eyes so that we could see the gifts and blessings he has for us. I remember the time my sister in law Lillie was on her death bed. She asked my other sister in law Edwina to call all the children in our family to come see her the day before she died. She was very sick and didn't say a whole lot. She asked all of them to pray always for wisdom every day from God and keep him first in their life. She knew that if they prayed for wisdom, they could solve any problem that would face them in the future. My children have never forgotten her words of wisdom. I know her words will bless our family for generations to come.

Scripture:

Proverbs 4:5-7
Get wisdom, get understanding: forget it not; neither decline from the words of my mouth. Forsake her not, and she shall preserve thee: love her, and she shall keep thee. Wisdom is the principal thing: therefore get wisdom; and with all thy getting get understanding.

Prayer:

Dear Lord,

Thank you for this day to praise you and give thanks for my children to have wisdom. Please forgive me for my sins and help me to forgive others who have sinned against me. Lord, in the name of Jesus, I speak your word into my children. I pray they will have supernatural wisdom, knowledge and common since, and that you be their source of divine wisdom in every area of their life. Protect them, save them by your grace, and give them a purpose by directing them and giving them divine wisdom. Thank you for blessing my family. I love you Lord.
Amen

12. God Delivers Us From Fear

I can hear my mother now asking me to go to bed. I was the youngest child and my bedtime was earlier then my siblings. I hated to go to bed. I had a fear of darkness and I remember staling every night when my parents said the words," Janice it is your bedtime." I had a fear of going to my room and being by myself while trying to go to sleep. My sisters and I shared a bedroom that was next to the kitchen. One way of getting there was to go through the kitchen. My mom had asked me several times to go to bed on this winter night. She started telling me at 8:30 to go and now it was almost nine o'clock. I had fallen asleep on the couch and I could hear the frustration in her voice telling me to go to bed. I was half asleep when I started walking to my room. My sisters were washing dishes and cleaning up the kitchen. As I walked in the kitchen, one of my sisters turned around with a pan of hot water. She was taking it to the sink. She ran into me and the water went all over me from my head to my feet. It woke me up and I remember not knowing what had happened. Water was all over me. Someone put a large towel around me. My mom put some medicine all over me. I remember my parents praying over me as I fell asleep. My parents felt it was time to address the fear I had. I told them I was afraid of the dark and hated going to bed by myself. They told me the scripture Proverbs 3:24, which reads (When thou liest down, thou shall not be afraid: yea, thou shall lie down, and thy sleep shall be sweet). I started trusting God to watch over me and his word comforted and delivered me from that fear. As I grew older I found there were other fears that would come. Mom always wrote my sister Diannah and me many speeches for us to learn for the 4-H talent shows. We had to learn and act out our speech. I had great fear right before I was to go on stage to say my speech. I then learn the scripture second Timothy 1:7 (For God hath not given us the spirit of fear: but of power, and of love and of a sound mind.) Mom had a talent for writing and because of the grace of God, we would always win first place in each one of our divisions.

Fear can torment and affect your body if it continues. Fear is not of God and should be replaced with faith. Prayer and learning scriptures are the best way for children to overcome fear. God's word is so powerful that when children learn these scriptures, they will be tucked away in their mind, and they remember to relax when fear tries to overtake them.

Scripture:

Romans 10:17
So then faith cometh be hearing, and hearing by the word of God.

Psalm 34:4
I sought the Lord, and he heard me and delivered me from all my fears.

Psalm 107:20
He sent his word, healed them, and delivered them from their destructions.

Prayer:

Dear Heavenly Father, In the name of Jesus we come to you lifting our children up and we rebuke and come against the spirit of fear and doubt. Your word says," (use any scripture about fear)"
We ask you to forgive us for all our sins and help us to forgive people who have hurt us. Today we speak to the fear our children have. We come against doubt and unbelief. My

children have confidence in themselves and fear has no place in their life. My children will rest in your word and it will give them great peace. Fear will not torment them. They will learn and stand on your word and relax and have faith when fear tries to overtake them. Thank you for your word that gives us a peach of mind. Help us not to fear but speak your blessings over them and have faith that they will overcome fear. We love you Lord.
Amen

13. I Need Time For Me

I have always felt that each day was an adventure. We make so many decisions every day. Some are good and some not so good. I found that if I start my day and end it with prayer, I will have peace knowing that everything will turn out ok. When my children were younger, I felt that 24 hours was not enough time to get everything in. I remember asking God to help me. I worked and tried to keep a clean house. I remember one night after the children had scripture, story and prayer time and were sleep; and I spent some time with my husband, I was exalted. I felt that I had given every minute of my day to my family, my church and my job. Somehow there was no time for me. I had no time to read a good book or take a long bubble bath and soak in the tub. There was no ME time. I remember asking God for help. One day I talked with my sister Norma and my sister in law Lillie and they both said," I know it is hard for you now, but you don't have to do everything in one day. God understands that you are one person not two. You can only do so much. If it doesn't get done today, add it to tomorrow. Don't stress yourself out when you can't do something. It is ok to say no I can't do that today. If you help to save everyone in your house, you will have done a lot in your life time. Your children are God's precious gift and giving up your time now will pay off later when they are older." She was right. The older and more independent they got, the more time I had for me. We were still busy but I could find a little time for me. Now when I see mothers with small children, I tell them," It's hard now, but it will get better!"

Scripture:

Acts 16:31
And they said, Believe on the Lord Jesus Christ, and thou shalt be saved, and thy house.

Prayer:

Dear Heavenly Father,

I come to you with thanksgiving. Thank you for giving me my children. When we are connected to you, you will provide everything we need. Thanks for giving me the time and the strength to take care of my family. Thank you that I can find time for me as well as my family. You have blessed and graced us to do great things. Please forgive our sins and help us to forgive others. Thanks for saving everyone in my house and thanks for loving us. I love you Lord!
Amen

14. In the Midst of the Storm (Faith)

I was so blessed to grow up in Oklahoma. There are many places in Oklahoma that are so beautiful. The people I grew up around were so nice and friendly. Oklahoma also has a lot of storms and tornados in the spring. This was a way for God to help the farmers to grow their crops. Everything is so beautiful and green in the spring and summer. There are many things in life that takes your breath away and the clean fresh air after a storm is one of them.

One evening we were listening to the T.V. and the weather man predicted that flash flood thunder storms and tornados were coming our way. My sister Diannah and I were frightened and asked our parents if we were going to go into town to get in my aunt and uncle's storm cellar. My dad looked at my mom and they both told us that we had been in many storms before and God had blessed our family through them all. Mom called us to the dinner table to eat dinner. We talked about our day as the rain began to come down. We cleaned up the kitchen after family dinner time and the storm seemed to be right on top of our farm. The hail stones were hitting the roof of our house. Then came the thunder and the lightning seem to flash through our windows. My sister and I looked at each other and said what are we going to do now? It was about 9:30 p.m. when my dad and mom called us to the dining room table. My sister and I expressed how afraid we were. My dad and mom were so calm, which made us, feel better but we were still afraid. My dad took the lead and told us that it was storming outside but God said to trust in him with all our heart and acknowledge him and he shall direct us. He then said we must trust God to protect us always and we must have faith that God will keep us in his care. When we worship God and have faith, his love and blessings will cover and keep us. We must think and speak victory for us to receive it. Then my father said," So right now girls we are going to pray and ask God to take care of us while we sleep. God is greater than any storm and everything against us. Tomorrow is a new day. We must rest and get ready for God to bless us. We prayed and agreed that God would protect us while we are sleeping. We went to bed and my sister and I listened to the sounds of the storm outside. It wasn't long before we fell asleep. The next morning, we woke up with the smell of eggs and bacon coming from the kitchen. We ran into the kitchen and mom gave us a big hug. My mom asked," Did you girls sleep good?" We said," yes", and sat down for breakfast. Dad was talking about the storm and the damage it brought to the farm. After breakfast, we went outside and the roof on one of our barns was half way off, but all our cattle were fine. Our storage house had a little damage. One of our tractors was lying on its side. The chicken house had some roof damage. The white rabbit cages were untouched. The pigs were fine. The biggest surprise was the big tree right behind our house. It was broken in half and lying on its side away from our house. Somehow the storm tore down things all around our farm but did not touch our house. This was an excellent example that no matter how bad the storm may be, God will protect and keep us if we have faith. My husband and I have been through many storms since then. We have tried to be an example and to teach our children that no matter what may come, faith is the power that moves mountains. When we speak positive into our negative, God will bless us to see our words become our victory.

When our children see us believing God for things we can't see they become life-long learners of trusting God for everything. To have faith is to have peace of mind. To have faith means we can't think negative or wrong thoughts about our situation. We must think above our situation. If satin can deceive us into thinking we can't be victorious, then we become what we think. Our thoughts are so powerful. That's why God said we would have perfect peace if we keep our mind on him.

Scripture:

Hebrews 11:1
Now faith is the substance of things hoped for, the evidence of things not seen.

Hebrews 11:6
But without faith it is impossible to please him; for he that cometh to God must believe that he is, and that he is a rewarder of them that diligently seek him.

Matthew 17:20
And Jesus said unto them, Because of your unbelief: for verily I say unto you, if ye have faith as a grain of mustard seed, ye shall say unto this mountain, remove hence to yonder place, and it shall remove, and nothing shall be impossible unto you.

Mark 11: 22-24
And Jesus answering saith unto them, Have faith in God. For verily I say unto you, that whosoever shall say unto this mountain, be thou removed, and be thou cast into the sea; and shall not doubt in his heart, but shall believe that those things which he saith shall come to pass, he shall have whatsoever he saith. Therefore, I say unto you, What things so ever ye desire, when ye pray, believe that ye receive them, and ye shall have them.

2 Corinthians 5:7
For we walk by faith, not by sight.

Prayer

Dear Heavenly Father,

Thank you for your word teaching us to have faith in you. We ask for forgiveness of our sins and for helping us to forgive those who have hurt us. Lord thank you that I can be an example for my children to walk in faith. I know that when my children pray the prayer of faith, nothing will be impossible for them. Lord we want to please you by stepping out on faith in every situation we face. We know that we see in the natural and you work in the supernatural. Please help us to walk by faith and not by what is going on with us. We praise and bless your holy name. Thank you, Lord Jesus.
Amen

15. Inner Healing For Your Child

As we grow and learn we experience many things. Many of our experiences become a part of our memory. The pleasant things that happen in our life become sweet memories. We laugh or smile when we play them back in our mind. We even tell our family and friends about them because we want to share our sweet thoughts. Parents often ask their children." How was your day?" We also ask our children," What did you learn today at school?" That is our way of getting them to share their thoughts with us. Many times our children experience hurtful things that they don't share. They try to keep it to themselves. They keep it bottled up because they didn't know how to handle a situation or they are embarrassed or is feeling failure. They could also be beating themselves up by replaying the situation in their mind and wishing they had said or done something differently. This can cause mental confusion. Let's compare your child's heart to a glass. When something disappointing happens to them that they don't share, their glass starts to fill. As things happen, their glass continues to fill up. If we keep pouring water in the glass, it will over flow and start to run out on the table. That's when we see the effect that something is wrong. We then try to clean up the water. The same thing happens with our children's heart. When a child come home looking sad, worried, or his behavior has changed, we know that something is wrong. His glass is full. Jesus is the one who can heal all our pains. He wants to heal our hurts and bad memories threw inner healing. Jesus wants to give us peace to replace our mental confusion. Sometimes they just need to talk and needs someone to listen. Before talking with your child, pray and ask the Holy Spirit to reveal to you what is going on with your child and what to say to him. Show him you are listening by having good eye contact. Explain to your child that to have inner peace, he is going to have to forgive the person or persons who have hurt him. He may need to talk with his friend.

Matthew 6:14-15 says "(14) for if ye forgive men their trespasses, your heavenly Father will also forgive you: (15). But if ye forgive not men their trespasses, neither will your Father forgive your trespasses."

Let him talk it through. When we keep replaying what hurt us in our mind, and not give it to God, the pain can last a long time. Jesus loves us very much. He wants us to have inner peace. There is no problem our Lord and Savior can't solve. When we give it to him, and don't take it back, he heals our pain. All of us may need inner healing some time in our life. To God be the glory for blessing us with inner healing and giving us joy and peace.

Scripture:

Philippians 4:7
And the peace of God, which passeth all understanding, shall keep your hearts and minds through Christ Jesus.

Ephesians 2: 14
For he is our peace, who hath made both one, and hath broken down the middle wall of partition between us;

Prayer:

Dear Heavenly Father

Lord we praise you and we love you. We ask for forgiveness for all of our sins. We thank you for your grace and mercy. Thank you for my child_____ who needs prayer and inner healing. Lord Jesus we all agree and ask that you go into _____ life and heal and clean every place that is hurting him right now. Heal him from all fears and gilt. Set him free from the pain he is feeling right now. We ask forgiveness for all our sins, step out on faith, and forgive those who have hurt him. Lord please take away any feeling of embarrassment and failure. Please set him free and repair the hurt. We know you can restore his confidence because he belongs to you. Thank you for replacing the bad memories with your peace. And Lord thank you for loving and saving us. This we ask in our Lord and Savior Jesus Christ's Name. AMEN

16. God is in Our Schools

I will never forget the feeling I had when I first held my children in my arms. Each child was a sweet and adorable miracle that God had given to Kenn and I. Joe was my husband's son by birth and I birthed Kenneth Damian, Shannon and Jamie. Nicole is my God baby. At the age of ten her mom, my sister Diannah died, and she became one of my children. There is a special feeling I get when I think of them all. I also have special nieces and nephews that I love and are dear to me. Children are the most unique and special gift you get from God. Naturally you want the best for them. When they were school age, I started praying that they would get a teacher who would love and respect them. I wanted a teacher who loved God. I was a public school teacher and I knew that in every school I worked, most of the teachers were Christians. I knew that many people put their children in private schools for assurance that they would get the best education. Every teacher I worked with was well trained and also was excellent educators. I wanted to make sure that my children got the right teacher who would make them feel happy to be there. So every year I prayed that they would get the right teacher. I taught school for over 25 years and was an elementary counselor for 10. Every day I prayed that the children in my classroom and my own children would get everything they needed. I respected each child and expected them to respect each other. At the end of every day I told my students individually as they left my room for home that I loved them. I noticed how powerful and important "I love you" was when a student went back to his desk for something he had forgotten. I thought everyone was gone. I was talking to another teacher across the hall when he walked out of the room and over to me. He stood waiting after the class had left for me to say "I love you". When I said it, he smiled, hugged me and ran to meet his mom. God has his people everywhere. He has them in public, private and home schools. He even has them in college and vocational schools. Oh what a wonderful God we serve. Jesus came to give our children life. They take him with them everywhere they go. We can't be with them all day but God is always with them. When we pray, his grace and favor covers them and they are blessed. Pray and ask God to answer you, and show you great and mighty thing concerning your children. Our conversations with God are rewarding and help us to have a worry free day. Just trust God and no matter where your child goes he or she will be blessed and safe.

Scripture:

Jeremiah 33:3
Call on me, and I will answer thee, and shew thee great and mighty things, which thou knowest not.

Psalm 107: 31
Oh that men would praise the Lord for his goodness, and for his wonderful works to the children of men!

Prayer:

Dear Lord, which art in Heaven we praise you. We glorify your holy name. We thank you for all the blessings that you give to us and our children. Thank you that we can call on you for anything concerning our family. Keep us in perfect peace when our children are at school or away from us knowing you are with them. Help us to forgive others and please forgive our sins. Help our children to make good choices and have the friends you want in their life. Help them to be good citizens and to love you with all of their hearts. We

ask the Holy Spirit to guide them in decision making and keep them safe from hurt, harm, and danger. Thanks that we can come to you anytime for guidance. We love you Lord!
Amen

17. Keep Praying Those Stains Will Come Out

Our children like us go through things all the time. Their problems may seem small to us but to them they are devastating. If we could walk in their shoes we would see things differently.

There have been behaviors I have seen in my children and the children at school that I felt would hurt them or have a bad outcome. I would talk with my own children and tell them, "lets pray about this. Give it to God and see how he will lead you", and then pray every time it came into my mind. Sometimes our prayers were answered quickly, and other times it took longer. There were times I would pray, and I knew God was listening and working on it, but I couldn't see what he was doing. I had faith and knew he had his hands on them, but I just couldn't see the outcome fast enough. I continued praying and speaking God's word on them knowing that Satan couldn't destroy them while God was answering my prayers.

One morning I woke up around 4:30 a.m. and couldn't get back to sleep. When this happens, it is time for me to get up and spend some time with Jesus. I really enjoy praying in my kitchen. I guess you could say that is my prayer closet. I like to walk around the island in the center of that room and just pray and bathe in the spirit. After praying, I noticed a pan I had put in the sink to soak covered with water. I knew by morning it would be easier to wash clean. I decided to go ahead and clean the pan. I noticed stains on the outside of the pan. I have been scrubbing this pan for years and had not been able to get those stains off that pan. God spoke to me and said," you have given up on restoring that pan back to the way it used to look". "You really don't believe you can get those stains out, so you clean the inside and put it away. You have given up. You have never scrubbed long and hard because you believe you can't get it clean." I got another cleaning pad and started scrubbing real hard. I could not believe it. That old pan was clean and restored and looked like new.

Then God said," that's the way prayer is. People pray for God to bless and answer prayers and when they don't see a change, they give up and think that's the way it is going to be." They stop expecting the stain to come out. We stop praying and feel defeated. If we trust God, WE TRUST GOD! If we have faith, we keep praying and thanking God until we see the stain come out. Just because we can't see what he is doing does not mean he isn't doing anything. Get into the word of God and scrub a little harder. Use another pad. Pray God's scriptures. Fast and have faith. Ask your children to pray with you. Those stains WILL COME OUT! God's word is your comforter. Your faith and speaking Gods word is your scouring pad. HIS WORD WILL NOT RETURN VOID. WE NEVER FAIL WHEN WE HAVE FAITH. We must decree and speak life into our situation. "Death and life are in the power of the tongue." (Proverbs 18:21)

Don't ever give up or worry about your children. Give them totally to God. Decree and speak that Satan can't have your children. It doesn't matter what the situation looks like. If you keep decreeing and believing in God, those stains will disappear, and God will supernaturally take care of your whole family.

Scripture:

Proverbs 18:21
Death and life is in the power of the tongue.

Proverbs 29:17
Correct thy son, and he shall give the rest: yea, he shall give delight unto thy soul.

Isaiah 54:13
And all thy children shall be taught of the Lord; and great shall be the peach of thy children.

Hebrews 11:1.6
Now faith is the substance of things hoped for, the evidence of things not seen. But without faith it is impossible to please him: for he that cometh to God must believe that he is and that he is a rewarder of them that diligently seek him.

Corinthians 5:7
For we walk by faith, not by sight.

Ephesians 6:11,13,18
Put on the whole armor of God that ye may be able to stand against the wiles of the devil. Wherefore take unto you the whole armor of God, that ye may be able to withstand in the evil day, and having done all, to stand. Praying always with all prayer and supplication in the spirit, and watching thereunto with all perseverance and supplication for all saints.

Philippians 4:6,7,9
Be careful for nothing; but in everything by prayer and supplication with thanksgiving let your requests be made known unto God. And the peace of God, which passeth all understanding, shall keep your hearts and minds through Christ Jesus. Those things, which ye have both learned, and received, and heard, and seen in me, do; and the God of peace shall be with you.

Jeremiah 33:3
Call unto me and I will answer thee, and shew thee great and mighty things, which thou knowest not.

Prayer:

Father in the name of Jesus I thank you. I love and adore you. Please forgive me if I have done or said anything that is not pleasing to you. Father please bless _____. I ask that your blessing and favor make _____ superior to his circumstances. Thank you for healing and delivering him from _____. I decree and believe that faith is the substance of things hoped for and the evidence of things not seen. They have divine protection and walk in total restoration in Jesus name.
Amen

18. Letters to My Lord

When I was a little girl the mailman would come every day to bring us our mail. I never got a letter, but I noticed my parents thinking it was a big deal. My mom would ask one of us to go to the mail box and get it after the mailman had left. I was in my teens when I got my first letter. It was from my cousins saying they couldn't wait to see me. Every other year Rick and Vincent would come all the way from Milwaukee with their parents to visit us for two weeks. I had such excitement when I opened the letter. I felt so important that they took the time to write me. Reading the letter was so exciting also. They talked about the last time they were here and wanted to know what we had planned for them this year. They came a few weeks later and we had a wonderful time on the farm. I got another letter from them a few weeks after they had gone home. That was another day of excitement for me when I opened my letter. They thanked me making them feel so special and for them having a good time. This made me feel so special and loved. I remember putting it in my drawer and getting it out from time to time to read. Every time I read it, I felt just as good as I did the first time I opened it.

One day when my children were small, I had so much going through my mind. I was praying for them and my husband like I always do, and I was wondering what I had prayed the day before. There was so much I needed to discuss with my Lord and I wanted to make sure I told him everything on my mind. I remembered the letters I got when I was a little girl and how it made me feel to receive them. Then I thought that if letters from people I love made me feel good then it would make my Lord feel good. That was when I started writing to my Lord. I got a journal and dated my letters every time I wrote to him. I found that it not only made me feel great to get what was on my mind down on paper to the Lord, but I could go back and read what was on my mind a certain day and I could also see that My God answered my prayers. It's funny that they were all answered but not all answered at the same time. How refreshing it was to see that God truly loves me and he cares more for me then I do for myself. Things that are important to me are also important to God. I noticed that he didn't work my situations out the way I would have but better. His ways are not our ways. His grace is free for the asking and money can't buy his favor. All he wants us to do is praise him and have faith that he will do it and he will. Thank you, Lord, for loving me!

Scripture:

Romans 8:28
And we know that all things work together for good to them who are called according to his purpose.

Matthew 19:26
But Jesus beheld them and said unto them. With men this is impossible; but with God all things are possible.

Prayer:

Dear heavenly Father. There is nothing impossible for you. You love your children and you answer our prayers. We thank you that we are able to call on you at any time. With you all things are possible and your word is the final authority in my family's life. My children's body is the temple of the holy spirit. Thank you for answering our prayers. Our children have the mind of Jesus and nothing shall be impossible unto them. We love you Lord.
Amen

19. Nothing is Impossible With God

I grew up on a farm. My parents had six children and I was the youngest of them all. There were many things I felt I could do because I saw my older sisters and brothers doing it. I really was too small to do some things but I tried it anyway because everyone else could do it. I was like a bumble bee. Scientifically it has been proven that the bumblebee cannot fly because his wingspan is too short. But the bumble bee can fly. Nobody knows why. I believe that we have victory by thinking we can, pray about it, and not giving up. That is stepping out on faith. When a baby is ready to walk, we encourage him to walk by stepping a few steps away and holding out our hands. He tries to walk and falls a few times but because we believe he can walk, he soon starts walking. God feel us with everything we need to be successful. So nothing is impossible with God. Encouragement and prayer makes anything possible. My daughter Jamie's soccer team was playing in a city tournament. They had won many games and lost a few but they were in the finals. Their team was so excited and really wanted to win because they had never been the city champs. We prayed and the team worked really hard to win. They won their last game and became the city champs. This was a good chance for us to explain that sometimes we win and sometimes we lose but if we have faith and work hard, our goal is not impossible.

Scripture:

Luke 1:37
For with God nothing shall be impossible.

Prayer:

Dear Heavenly Father: You are a great God and you made each one of us. Thank you for all of your blessings. Thank you for giving my children special talents. Thank you for helping them to be good winners and good losers. Please forgive us of all our sins and help us to forgive others who have hurt us Thank you for your goodness mercy and grace. We love you very much. Amen

20. The Balls You Throw Are the Balls You Get Back

Have you ever heard the expression "You never know love until you give it"?

When I was a first-grade teacher, I had many children come to me to tell what their friend had done to them, but they left out what they did to their friend. In discussing the situation, I found out that both students really felt that the other one had done them wrong. As the conversation went on both students would argue that the other one started it. They felt that the person who started it was the one who should get in trouble and not them. Even though they participated in the disagreement, it was not their fault and their feelings were hurt. They were very unhappy. Many people say words to others but when those same words are said back to them, they find them very offensive. When we are angry, and our adrenaline starts to flow in our body, we sometimes don't hear what we are saying to others because we are so angry.

Teaching children to think before they react is sometimes difficult to explain. I found that using a ball can help them to realize that what they say to others comes back to them. I start off be throwing a ball to the child. As I am throwing the ball I say positive words for example," You are so nice". Then ask the child to throw the ball back to you and tell him to repeat what you have said. " You are so nice". Throw the ball again and say," It is fun playing with you". Have the child to repeat what you have said, and he throws the ball back to you and say," It is fun playing with you". Now say something that is not positive and throw the ball. "You are not nice". Have the child to throw the ball back and say those exact words. "You are not nice". Throw the ball again and say." I don't like you". Have the child to return the ball and say, "I don't like you". You may use any example you choose to get your point across. It is important to treat others the way you want to be treated. If you treat others with respect, you will get respect returned to you. If you say unkind words to others, you will get those unkind words returned to you.

All children want to have friends and to be liked. It does not matter if you are tall or short or what color your skin is. It does not matter how big or little you are. The color of your hair or eyes does not make a difference. God made us all and we are all important. Every person is special and dear to God. When you love your friends, you will feel God's love returned to you.

Scripture:

John 15:12
This is my commandment, that you love one another, just as I have loved you.

Prayer:

Dear Lord: Thank you for your grace and mercy concerning my children. Thank you for my children. Thank you for the love we have for each other. Help my children to have friends and to be a friend to others. Help them to respect their friends and for that same respect to be returned to them. Help them to have favor wherever they go. Bless them to have wisdom knowledge and common sense. Help them to make good decisions. Thank you, Lord, for your grace over my children. In Jesus' name we pray.
Amen

21. Sticky Situation

I woke up early one Sunday morning thinking of all the things that had to be done before we would leave for church. After getting my thoughts together I got out of bed and started my day. I picked out the clothes my children were going to wear to church and I cooked breakfast. My husband Kenneth got everyone up and they all came to the table to eat. When breakfast was over, we started getting ready for church. That's when I noticed that one of my daughters had a large hard sticky piece of gum in her hair. I tried to get it out but the harder I pulled the more tangled it got. I was in a hurry. I got so frustrated because no matter what I did, I couldn't get the gum out. I knew if I were to cut it out, her hair would be uneven and look horrible. We prayed together about the situation and gave it to God. My mom called, and I told her about my problem. It was getting late and I felt I would not make it to church on time. She told me to get some peanut butter and mix it with the gum that was in her hair. I did, and I noticed that I could easily pull the gum out. I quickly washed her hair and all of the gum was gone. I felt a sense of calmness when it was all over. We made it to church and ended up having a wonderful day.

There are many situations that come up every day. Some problems are easy, and some are hard to solve. Our children like us, have to make many decisions every day. Sometimes they can find themselves in a sticky situation and not know what to do. Some problems may seem too difficult to work out. It can be very frustrating for them. Their attitude may change, or you may find them in deep thought. They may seem distant or unhappy. Stop what you are doing and pray a short prayer for them. Seeing you pray when you face situations helps them to know what to do. Pray about everything with your children. They are great prayer partners. Write down your prayer request in a journal. Go back weeks later and show them how wonderful God is and that he does answer prayers. Shannon tried out for cheerleader in high school. I was so excited when she told me that some of her friends got together and prayed with her to make the squad. Everyone was so happy and excited when she made it. They started praying for each other about other things each one was facing. They are still friends today. You will not always be with your child when they are faced with a sticky situation, but God is always there. When they ask you," what should I do", tell them let's go to God in prayer and find out what he wants you to do. He will lead you and help you to make the right decision every time.

Scripture:

Isaiah 26:3
Thou wilt keep him in perfect peace whose mind is stayed on thee: because he trusteth in thee.

Psalm 37:4
Delight thyself also in the Lord: and he shall give thee the desires of thine heart.

Mark 11:24
Therefore I say unto you, What things soever ye desire, when ye pray, believe that ye receive them, and ye shall have them.

Prayer:

Father, in the name of Jesus, We thank you for your perfect peace and the power of your precious word. We thank you that we can call on you anytime of the day and you will give us the desires of our heart. Lord please be merciful unto my

children.   Help them to trust and have faith in you for all things. Thank you, Lord that they trust in you for total victory in every situation they face. I decree and declare that they win every spiritual battle they face. They are winners in Jesus name.
Amen

22. Texas Move

When we moved to Dallas Texas in 1982, we bought a house for our family. I loved the neighborhood. We had found a church home at Mt. Pisgah Baptist Church. In November, I started teaching first grade at a school near my home. It wasn't long before school was out in May. We decided to put a swimming pool in our back yard. We really enjoyed it. We had never had a pool so this was very exciting for our family. We soon put our children in swimming lessons. It was fun to come home and practice what we had learned in the lessons. One day we had been swimming in the shallow part of the pool. Kenneth came home so I pulled everyone out. I needed to check on our dinner. I asked everyone to sit down in a chair on the porch to dry off and not get up. They promised me they would not get out of their lawn chair. I ran in and checked to food. On my way out, Damian ran in the house and said that Shannon had fallen in the pool. Ken was coming down the hallway and I told him that Shannon had fallen in the pool. We all ran out to the pool and she was in the 9-foot area. Kenneth jumped into the water and pushed her to the edge. I pulled her out and checked to see if she was okay. She was fine. We dried her off and we all sat down for a little talk. We asked them to tell us what happened. Why didn't they stay on the porch for those two minutes? Kenneth Damian told us that he and Shannon were playing tug of war. They kept moving toward the pool and finally Shannon fell in. They didn't mean to get off the porch. It was an accident. We had a long talk and they all were grounded from the pool for a week. We talked about the danger of them not listening and following directions. I told them that God was so good to us. He protected Shannon while Damian got help. Damian said" yes, he did but I think he wanted to teach her a lesson because she kept going down and up and down and up in the water". I reminded him that Shannon wasn't the only one who got off the porch. I think all of us learned a lesson that day. I told them from now on when I go in the house, we all go in the house.

Scripture:

Proverbs 4:7
Wisdom is the principal thing; therefore get wisdom: and with all thy getting get understanding.

Job 22:28
Thou shall also decree a thing, and it shall be established unto thee: and the light shall shine upon thy ways.

Prayer:

Father in the name of Jesus, I thank you for your goodness, mercy, grace, and your divine protection over my family. By the grace of God, I decree your word over my children that they are safe and protected from all hurt harm and danger. Help us to be the parent you want us to be over our children. Give us wisdom, knowledge and common since when making decisions over them. Thank you for the many miracles you do for us seen and unseen. I declare that they are safe and protected. When our children come to us with a problem, help us to tell them," let's go to God in prayer, and ask for his direction". Thank you for your peace, and supernatural power in the name of Jesus we pray.
Amen

23. Thank You Lord For My Children

We determine what kind of day we will have. "Don't start your day until you pray." That is our family slogan. The way we start our day determines how our day will go. Even in the midst of a storm we can stop and pray to change our situation. Every day is a new start for us. If you don't believe in yourself, you can't be successful. Having a good self-esteem is a learned behavior. Tell your child to look in the mirror and say. "I love Me". Tell them to walk tall with their head up and not down. People with low self-esteem walk with their head down and are not self-confident. We should stop looking at what we are not and look at who and what we are. We are a child of the most high God. We belong to Jesus. If you decide you are happy, you will be happy. If you decide you are sad that day, you will be. What we think on the inside is what people will see on the outside. If your child has self-love, others will see his outstanding qualities and love him. Make a point to tell your child every day, "THANK YOU LORD FOR (your child's name)." This lets them know that you love and respect them and you thank God for them. It also re-affirms that God is the head of our house. What a blessing you will bring to your children.

Scripture:

Mark 11:24
Therefore I say unto you, What things so ever ye desire, when you pray, believe that ye receive them, and ye shall have them.

Jeremiah 29:11
For I know thoughts that I think toward you, saith the Lord, thoughts of peace, and not of evil, to give you an expected end.

Prayer:

Dear Lord: We thank you for this day. Please forgive us for our sins and help us to forgive others. We are asking that you perfect the things that concerns my children and our family. We cast all our cares on you for we know you care for us. Please put a hedge of protection around my children and my family. My children are the head and not the tail. They are witty, have common since, and make good decisions. They choose friends that are good citizens and make good decisions. Bless our family and friends. Help us all to have a good day. We are anointed to live this life, and God is the strength of my life. We love you Lord Jesus.
A-men

24. Plead the Blood of Jesus

I was blessed to grow up on a farm in Oklahoma. Some nights I would wake up and I would see my dad at the kitchen table reading his bible and I would listen to him pray. He would always plead the blood of Jesus over us and the farm. He also asked the angels to watch over us. I didn't realize how important that was until I was grown and had a family of my own. I was the youngest of six children. We never got bitten by a snake or hurt by anything all the years while growing up.

One evening I went to get the cows to be milked. My dad told me they were in the pastor across the road from my house on my grandparent's land. I went down to the creek and they were not there. I looked high and low and couldn't find them. Finally, I went to my grandparent's house and there they were in the field beside their house. I was tired and upset because I had to go so far to find them. I said the cow call and started walking towards them. I was looking down to make sure I was not stepping on anything and when I looked up all 60 head of cattle were running toward me. I could not believe my eyes. I couldn't run to the right or left to get out of their way because they were running to fast. All I could do was to cover my eyes. I could hear cows running on each side of me but did not open my eyes. A minute later the sound was gone. I turned around to see all sixty cows running home. When I got home, I told my dad about it. Then I told my family during dinner what had happened. My mom said that it was an angel that stepped in front to stop those cows from trampling me. My eyes were closed. I didn't see the angel, but I knew I could have been dead and an angel saved my life.

Scripture:

Psalm 91:11
For he shall give is angels charge over thee, to keep thee in all thy ways.

Prayer:

Dear Heavenly Father: Thank you, Lord, for your loving kindness. We bless your Holy Name. I plead the blood of Jesus over my children. Thank you for sending your Angels to watch over and help us. Thank you for putting a hedge of protection around my family. Please forgive us for all our sins. I will praise thee always. How excellent is your precious name?
Amen

25. Trouble in Paradise

It was a beautiful spring day. I always look forward to Saturday. The day started out ok, but as it went on my husband and I had a disagreement. He was upset, and I was upset and before long we both stopped listening to what the other person was saying. We decided we were angry and we both had nothing else to say. We were trying not to be in the same room with each other. We were walking around the house trying to make sure the other knew we were upset. It wasn't long before I noticed that our children were not having a good day either. They were arguing and saying things to each other that was not pleasant. We were trying to referee little argument and finally I felt that I have had enough. We sat them down and gave them a chance to talk about what was going on. After ten minutes of conversation, one of our children said, "you and dad aren't getting along either so why are you picking on us for not getting along?" WOW! That hit me like a ton of bricks. I couldn't disagree because it was true, and they knew it. Ken and I looked at each other and I had to do some quick thinking. I had to call on Jesus, so I said a quick short prayer in my mind and asked God to help us with this situation. God always comes through. We had to own up to the fact that we were not getting alone but we did say," that does not mean that we don't love each other". They said, "we love each other also but sometimes we feel the same way that you and dad feel and don't want to be around each other." Ken and I looked at each other and I spoke to Jesus again in my mind. "Jesus, where are you? HELP!" Then out of the blue, Kenn said," you are so right. We didn't know you were aware of what was going on between us. We are sorry. Your mom and I will talk and work this out. In the mean time you children must work out your problems so we can have a good day. Then I said," you know we determine what kind of day we are going to have. We can't get angry with someone unless we allow ourselves to do so. We all need to control our emotions." Let's start this day again. We apologized and made them apologize to each other. The rest of the day was so much better. We ended up having a wonderful Saturday. Children watch their parents. When we say and do things, that gives them permission to do it because we are their example. Raising our children is a big responsibility. They listen to the words that come out of our mouth. They observe our good and bad habits. They watch how we dress. They look at how we treat others. They love and respect and try to be us. Ken and I still have our disagreements from time to time, but they didn't know it. We kept that between us as it should be. We take turns letting each other win and tried to have respect and balanced emotions for each other's opinion. God will give you wisdom and show you great and mighty things if you ask, pray, trust him, and have faith.

Scripture:

James 1:5
If any of you lack wisdom, let him ask of God, that giveth to all men liberally, and upbraided not; and it shall be given him.

Proverbs 15:1
A soft answer turneth away wrath: but grievous words stir up anger.

Ephesians 4:31-32
Let all bitterness, and wrath, and anger, and clamour, and evil speaking be put away from you, with all malice; And be ye kind one to another, tenderhearted, forgiving one another, even as God for Christ's sake hath forgiven you.

Prayer:

Dear Heavenly Father, we praise your holy name. We love you. Thank you God for your tender mercy and grace for my family. Jesus I ask that you bless my children and our home. Help me to be a good parent. Please forgive us for all our sins and help us to forgive others. Father help my children to love and respect each other. Help them to overcome all circumstances that come into their life. Please give me wisdom and knowledge when making decisions for them. Please give them wisdom, and help them to grow reading your word. Thank you for watching over them day and night and keeping them from danger. I love you Lord.
Amen

26. Picture This

When Kenn and I got married we waited a few years before we decided to have children. When we made the decision to start our family, we prayed for months, but nothing happened. We went to the Dr. to get advice. We tried all of those things but nothing happened. I prayed with my mom Valaska Pettus and she told me to pray a specific prayer asking for God to bless us with children. My dad Jesse Pettus told me to find a specific scripture in the bible and pray that scripture. He said that God's word is his will for us. The scripture I stood on was John Chapter 14, verse 15.I asked God for my children and I told him that I would give every child he gave back to him. I went to him for every situation and prayed for guidance in raising those children. He let me birth three children (Kenneth, Shannon, and Jamie) and we had one child that Kenn had before our marriage Joe, and Nicole my god daughter. That made five children. We were blessed. There were many situations that came up in their lives that needed guidance from God. I decided one day to take a picture of all of our family and individual pictures of our children and place them in my bible. (Example) If we needed wisdom, I put the picture in the book of Proverbs. I felt that if we covered our children with the word, and they spoke the word, they would be blessed.

If you pick up one of my bibles, you may see my family and extended family pictures all through it. We are a praying family.

Scripture:

John 14:13-14
Whatever you ask in My name, that will I do, so that the Father may be glorifies in the Son. If you ask Me anything in My name, I will do it.

Mark 11:24-25
Therefore I say to you, all things for which you pray and ask, believe that you have received them, and they will be granted you. But if you do not forgive, neither will your Father who is in heaven forgive your transgressions.

Prayer:

Dear Lord, Thank you for all of your blessings. Thank you for my children. Please forgive me for all of my sins and help me to forgive others. Thank you that I can come to you for all things concerning my children. Lord, in the name of Jesus I am believing your word that you are blessing them in everything they need right now. Thank you Lord that I can give everything to you and have peace of mind knowing you got this. I love you Lord. Amen

27. God Took Care of Us All

There is always lot to do from sun up to sun down on the farm. It was a beautiful hot summer morning. My sister and I were home from Langston U. and both of us had summer jobs in town. My sister Diannah worked at city hall and I was a teacher's assistant at Watonga grade school. My mom worked at the Senior Citizen Center teaching cooking and art classes. Before breakfast we prayed for God to bless our day and the three of us left to go into town for work. Every summer my cousins Lamont and Ervin from OKC would come to help my dad. They stayed across the road with my grandmother and would come to our house every morning for the day to help Dad. This morning Lamont and dad were working the fields on our other land, which was 2 miles away from our home. My grandmother needed Ervin to help her that day. My Dad left on the John Deere and Lamont was driving the ford tractor.

Every year local farmers would hire men with combines from other towns to help them with their crops. We had our own combine, so my dad never hired these men. Little did we know that some men were watching our routine. After dad and Lamont left, Ervin started to walk across the road to my grandmother 's house. Two men in a truck grabbed Ervin and put him in their truck. They drove to our other land to steal our combine. Dad and Lamont stopped at a neighbor's farm before going to the field. The men parked at the gate to our land. One of the men got out of the truck, walked across the dam, and up to the field where the combine was. The other man stayed in the truck with Ervin. He drove our combine down to the dam and started to drive across. The combine was too big to drive across the dam. Cars and trucks could go across but not a big combine. My dad would always drive the combine further down the road to our other gate to enter the field where we harvested our wheat. The combine started to slide down one side of the dam into the pond. The man in the truck jumped out to help his friend. Ervin jumped out the truck and ran toward home. He ran into Dad and Lamont. He told my dad his story and they drove to the dam. The men were gone, and the combine was half way in the water. We were so blessed and thankful that Ervin was safe and not hurt. My dad's neighbors helped him get his combine back to the field. God protected us and kept us from all hurt harm and danger.

We had many blessings that day. God watched over all of us. My mom, sister and I were not home when the men came. Ervin was safe with my dad and Lamont. My grandmother was safe, and the men didn't get my dad's new combine. They were never seen again.

Scripture:

Luke 10:19
Behold I give you power to tread on serpents and scorpions, and over all the power of the enemy, and nothing shall by any means hurt you.

Proverbs 3:5,6
Trust in the Lord with all thine heart; and lean not unto thine own understanding. In all thy ways acknowledge him, and he shall direct thy paths.

Prayer

Almighty Lord, You are faithful in all things. Thank you for your grace and mercy. We know we don't live in a perfect world. We know that everything will turn out for our good if we trust and have faith in you. Thank you that we can seek your guidance in all things and you will direct us. We ask you

to forgive and bless us and those who have hurt us. Thank you for covering us with the blood of Jesus.
Amen

28. In the Name of Jesus

It was a hot summer Saturday evening. Every evening all the children on our street would go outside to ride their bikes, skate boards, skates or just play ball. On this special Saturday Joe, Kenneth Damian, Shannon and Jamie were riding their bikes up and down our street. Kyle and Kline, and three other girls who lived on our street were also riding their bikes. There is another street that runs down a hill into my street. My house is at the bottom of the hill facing that street. The children enjoyed riding up and down that hill on their bikes as well as riding on the street where we live. For some reason Jamie and Kenneth decided to ride each other's bike down this hill. They thought it would be a lot of fun to ride without their shoes. As they were riding down the hill Jamie noticed that the brakes on Kenneth Damian's bike had stopped working. The bike had picked up a lot of speed. She stepped on the breaks several times, but the bike would not slow down. She was headed with great speed down to our street. At the same time a car turned onto our street from the right and was driving very fast. The driver did not see Jamie and continued his speed. I was washing dishes and looking out my kitchen window. I saw Jamie coming very fast down this hill and about to run into my street. I looked to my right and saw that car driving very fast. They were about to collide. I screamed "IN THE NAME OF JESUS THAT CAR WILL NOT HIT JAMIE."

I ran to the front door and ran outside. As I looked, I saw that car pass and right behind it flew Jamie on that bike. She finally got the bike to stop. We all were very happy. It scared Jamie and the whole family. Jamie said," I don't know what happened, but my bike somehow slowed down and rolled into the street right after that car had passed." We all knew what happened. We had just witnessed a miracle. When we trust in God's word, believe it, and have faith, "**HE WILL GIVE OUR CHILDREN DIVINE PROTECTION**".

Scriptures:

Job22:28
Thou shalt also decree a thing, and it shall be established unto thee; and the light shall shine upon thy ways.

John 16:23
 Verily, I say unto you, whatsoever ye shall ask at the Father in my name, he will give it you.

Mark 9:23
Jesus said to him, if you can do anything? Everything is possible for the person who believes!

Prayer:
Dear Heavenly Father, I love you. Please forgive me if I have done or said anything not pleasing to you. I thank you and praise you Lord for your love and your Divine Protection over my children. Thank you for your goodness mercy and grace over them. Help my children to make good decisions. Thank you for keeping them safe from all hurt harm and danger, and in your care. Send your angels to watch over them. I decree that my children are blessed, and they will overcome any and everything by the blood of the lamb. I thank you again. Amen

About the Author

Janice Pettus Manous grew up on a dairy, cotton and wheat farm in Watonga Oklahoma and has lived in Carrollton, Texas over 30 years. She is an Elementary school teacher and certified school counselor. She is married to Ken Manous and have five children Joe, Kenneth, Shannon, Jamie, and Nicole, and five grandchildren. She is a member of Mt. Pisgah Baptist church.